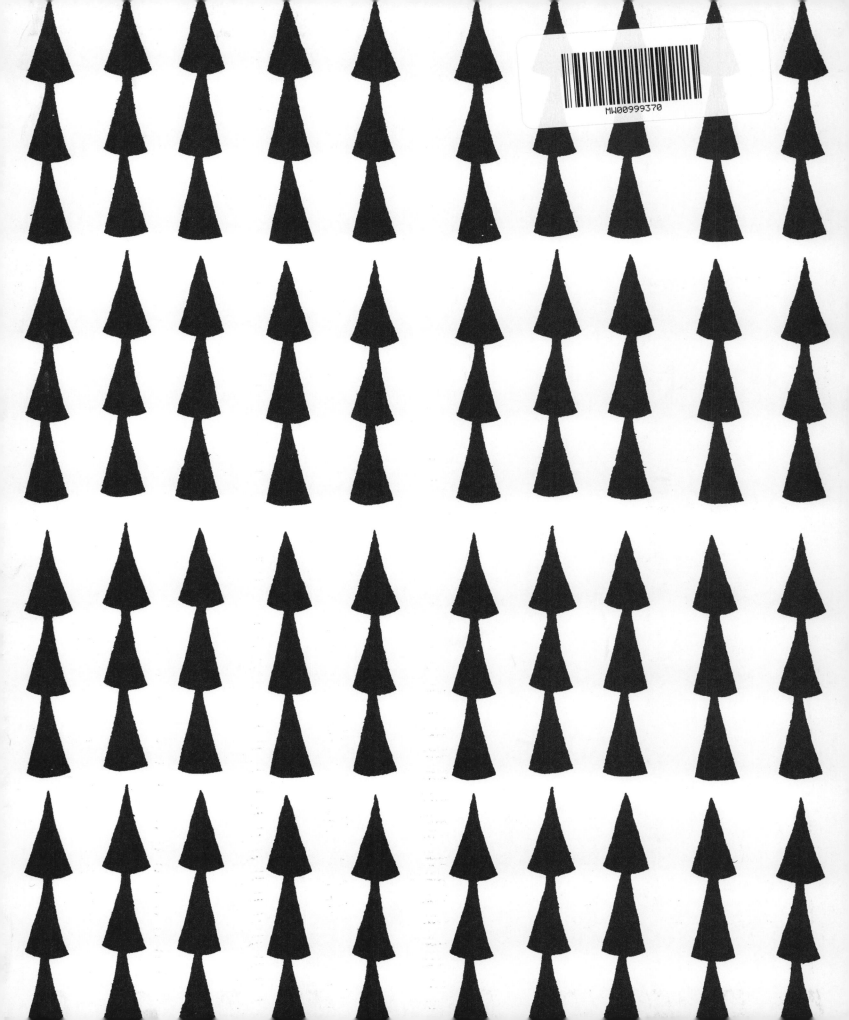

Lotta
Jansdotter

HANDMADE LIVING

Lotta Jansdotter

HANDMADE LIVING

A Fresh Take on Scandinavian Style

By Lotta Jansdotter

Photographs by Jenny Hallengren

CHRONICLE BOOKS
SAN FRANCISCO

ACKNOWLEDGMENTS

Jenny—it simply cannot be better!
TACK FÖR ALLT DITT FANTASTISKA JOBB.

Nerissa, Annika, Eri, and Sara—I appreciate your contribution
and help immensely. Thank you.

The ladies at Chronicle Books—Thank you for giving me the
chance to share my ideas and thoughts, over and over again, with
great patience and support.

Nick—all the "thank-yous" in the world are not enough.

Webster—there is nobody sweeter.

Tuesday—Arigato gozaimasu.

Many thanks and "GOD JUL" to—Matteo, Chiara, Jeremy, Patty,
Steve, Edith, Cole, Matt, Breck and Greta

I would like to dedicate this book to my dear husband, Nick,
who really is the best roommate I will ever have.
Tack Älskling!

Text copyright © 2010 by Lotta Jansdotter.
Photographs copyright © 2010 by Jenny Hallengren.
Illustrations copyright © 2010 by Lotta Jansdotter.

Library of Congress Cataloging-in-Publication Data available.
ISBN: 978-0-8118-6547-0

Manufactured in China

Designed by Tuesday
Styling by Lotta Jansdotter

10 9 8 7 6 5 4 3 2 1

Chronicle Books LLC
680 Second Street
San Francisco, California 94107
www.chroniclebooks.com

CONTENTS

INTRODUCTION

When I think about Scandinavian Style, I think of simplicity, functionality, and unpretentious classic forms. Today the term *Scandinavian Style* generally describes furniture and interior designs that first appeared in the 1930s and reached mass and international markets in the 1940s and '50s. Midcentury Scandinavian designers made use of natural materials and relied on traditional craft principles to create high-quality pieces with a handmade feel that would last for generations. The result is a style that is classic, elegant, and modern.

I was born on an island called Åland, and grew up in Sweden. For most of my life I was surrounded by simple, practical furnishings and timeless designs. So it's no surprise that many of these influences show up in my home now.

In my own home in Brooklyn, I've taken a very simple approach to decorating: functional, easy, organized, and not overly ornate. I like using pieces made from wood and natural fibers, things that have a timeless feel. My personal "Scandinavian Style" also incorporates touches of Asia and the West Coast, influences I picked up during my many travels to Japan and living in San Francisco for twelve years.

Ever since I was a little girl, I've been a real nester. I have a strong drive to decorate and create my own space. I love the challenge of an empty room—a nice clean slate—and I also constantly try to rearrange things in already settled rooms to update their look and feel.

I am not a big spender when it comes to furniture and accessories. Sure, it would be nice to have a set of Hans Wagner chairs around the dinner table, but at the moment that is not really a priority. Instead, I combine plain but practical pieces from Ikea with unique items from yard sales that add personality and style to my environment. I'm forever in search of garage sales and flea markets to hunt for useful, pretty, and inexpensive items to use around the house.

I also look for handmade pieces from independent and emerging artisans and designers. I'm lucky enough to have participated in a lot of trade shows and crafts fairs over the years, and I've been introduced to talented people who make gorgeous one-of-a-kind goods, many of which I keep in my home.

When it comes to decorating, I also like to make things myself. It's satisfying to sew my own curtains, print a set of pillows for the sofa, or throw my own tea cups on the pottery wheel. Having your own creations around the house is the best way to build a home that reflects your personal style.

In this book, I've opened up the doors to our three-bedroom apartment in Brooklyn, where I have lived for several years with my husband Nick, our two-year-old son August, and Webster, our big fat cat. We love this apartment for its open floor plan, all the wonderful natural light it gets, and its little balcony. Of course, someday I hope to have a bit more living space (and I could do without that four-story walk up every day), but for now this is the place we happily call home.

I'll give you a tour of how we live and how I've decorated my space. You'll spot influences from Scandinavia and notice my love of simple forms and timeless design pieces. You'll also notice a Bohemian touch, which stems from my time living in San Francisco. I like to use worn and used pieces in all different styles and from different eras, as well as combine many different materials and patterns. I love to mix things up—it's almost like creating an interior collage for my home.

We'll also take a peek at my second home—my office—to get a sense of how I design my workspace and find inspiration.

You'll find crafts projects and decorating tips throughout this book. I've included suggestions for items that you can easily make yourself. You won't find step-by-step instructions in this book since most of the crafts projects are so easy to do, but I have included a resources list to give you some guidance and clue you in to where I shop for my art and crafts supplies. To round things out, I've also included some of my secrets for entertaining, and creative ideas for holiday decorations and meals.

For me, home is not really home unless there is a bit of cooking involved, so I'll share some of my favorite Scandinavian recipes with you. You'll find some little recipe cards at the back of the book that you can remove (so as not to get the book covered with butter stains). The recipes are nothing fancy, nothing strange, just simple dishes that are easy to make and that say "home" to me.

It's my aim to show you that living a stylish life does not require a lot of money. It simply takes some interest, patience, and a touch of creativity. I hope you will find inspiration in the pages that follow to create a home that you love.

AT HOME

AT HOME

Living in New York can be stressful and draining at times. It's a busy, bustling place with a lot going on—all the time! We are also a family that stays busy with activities, travel, and, of course, work, so it's important to carve out time in our lives to take a few breaks and relax. I believe it is important to have a home that is warm and welcoming. We strive to have a home that is comfortable, relaxing, and organized, which can be tough when there are toys spread out everywhere, socks and T-shirts scattered on the bedroom floor, and dust bunnies hiding in the corners. But that is just life. As long as you do your best to keep things orderly and practical, home can be an escape from chaos (rather than a source of it!). As you'll see, we don't have a lot of space (I dream about storage closets and a basement), but we still manage to keep things relatively well maintained to suit our daily needs.

LIVING ROOM

Back home in Sweden, I spent a great deal of time at my grandmother's apartment, where we would all gather in the living room and play games, do puzzles and homework, watch television, and enjoy snacks. The living room was the heart of my grandmother's home, so now that I have my own family, I find I like to spend most of my time in our living room.

Since our Brooklyn apartment has a partially open floor plan (the kitchen is combined with the living room and eating area), we don't exactly have a living *room,* but we'll call it that for the sake of this book.

This room is where we watch movies, eat meals, read books to August, do work on our laptops, and generally spend most of our time. I'm actually very happy about the fact that the kitchen is combined with our living room—this way I can socialize, watch a TV show, or hang out with my family while I'm cooking. It's perfect!

One priority for our living room was having a place for guests to sleep, since we don't have a guest room and tend to get a lot of visitors (we live in New York, after all). We needed a sleeper sofa, but unfortunately they are not available in the sleek and slim midcentury style we had hoped for. Consequently our sofa bed is pretty big and chunky, but it is comfortable and accommodates one or two overnight guests.

Now, don't ask me what we were thinking when we got an off-white couch just before our first child was born. I admit it wasn't a very practical move. Today I would go with dark brown leather. You can just imagine all the stains and mishaps we've had, but we solve that by covering the couch with a white cotton blanket I bought in Shanghai, or with one of my handmade quilts.

ACCENTS

The shelving unit behind our couch is an assembly of pieces from Ikea with some other nice, sleek brackets and shelves that look more expensive than they really are. They fit so perfectly along that wall that they look custom made. These shelves are where I store our CD collection and books. They are simple and functional and their simplicity harmonizes with our style.

I like to collect trinkets and treasures—pieces that feel special, pretty, and unique. I then like to use them to set up "scenes" in different spots—sort of like still lifes, which I keep on display for a while. After a while I switch things up, and I rotate items and colors pretty frequently.

An easy way to create a scene like this is to group things together by color: simply make arrangements of items that are of similar colors. Another approach is to mix and match pieces that are varying shapes and sizes but relate to each other by material (such as a group of wooden pieces, or a gathering of glass vases in fun shapes).

It is very hard for me to pass a yard sale without having a peek—I always feel I just might find a special item that would perfectly fit in our home. I have to be very selective, though, because of our space limitations. Otherwise I might have to have my own yard sale soon!

Our dinner table was designed and built by my husband, Nick. Not only is it very stylish and the perfect size for our little family, but it also has an extra shelf underneath where I can store serving plates and extra knickknacks.

Our three large living room windows let in a lot of natural light, so it seemed a shame to cover them up. At the same time, our neighbors can see straight in, so we definitely needed curtains. To make some, I used three different kinds of fabric: plain cotton in the middle, opaque enough to give us privacy; sheer fabric higher up on the curtain to let light in; and on the bottom, a nice thick velvet that adds weight and a splash of color.

When we want the curtains open but still want some privacy, we use a simple, nifty cover that I made, a sort of mini folding screen. It's just a big sheet of matte cardstock, folded into an accordion pleat, which can easily be folded up and stored.

Felt is such a great material to work with and is easy to use to make accents for the home. I made this wonderful mobile, inspired by a design I saw in a Japanese magazine, from a big piece of industrial felt (industrial felt is thicker and sturdier than regular felt, so it worked well for this project). I also found some felt furniture pads in a hardware store that made excellent berries to add to the mobile. Furniture pads come in all kinds of sizes and a few different colors, and they have an adhesive on one side, so they can easily be stuck to a felt mobile (or anything else).

Kråkes Kök | Kråke Lithander

HUSHÅLLSLÄRA FÖR SKOLA OCH HEM

THE FANNIE FARMER COOKBOOK

PAOLO ROBERTO Mina favoriters mat

Leslie Mackie's MACRINA BAKERY & CAFE COOKBOOK

Bergenström KÄRLEK, OLIVER OCH TIMJAN

Underneath the shelving, I keep a basket where we can leave our bags (and August's shoes), so they won't lie scattered across the floor. It's a simple way to make use of space that otherwise would be wasted.

Most homes have awkward nooks or small spaces that are challenging to utilize. In this odd empty niche next to our entry door, we added more shelving, which gives us much needed storage for glassware, magazines, and cookbooks.

One of my favorite ways to change the tone of a room is to simply change its soft goods. Make textiles do the hard work for you. Switch out cushions and curtains. Use different patterns and colors. It is astonishing how different a room feels with pink accents rather than with green. This is the simplest and most economical way to update the look of a room. Luckily, pillowcases are really easy to sew yourself!

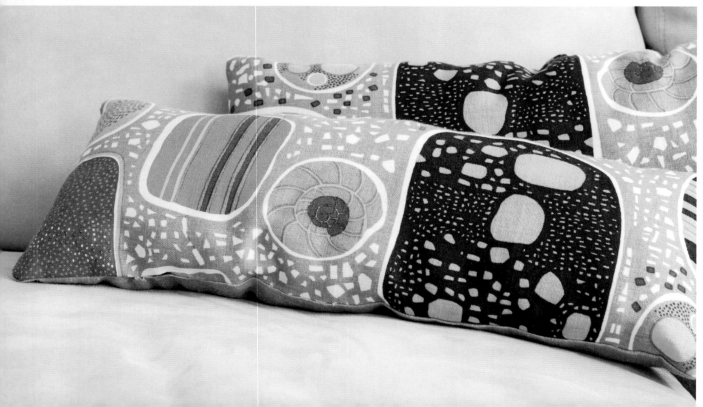

Because I am a textile designer, it probably is not surprising that I favor using lots of different fabrics in my everyday life. Using (and changing) fabric is such an easy way to decorate. Sure it takes some effort to do the washing and ironing, but it is so worth it. Fabric adds warmth. Patterns and colors add different moods and feelings.

The dining room is one place that's especially great for using textiles. I have a lot of different tablecloths and fabric napkins that I switch out regularly to keep our dining area fresh and vibrant. You can find fabrics and linens in so many different places. Keep an eye out at flea markets and rummage sales for unique and antique linens. Or buy fabric remnants—they're usually sold at a discounted price and can

be used to make great mix-and-match napkins! When I'm back home in Sweden, I visit my favorite fabric stores in hopes of finding special new fabric designs.

As far as caring for these kinds of fabrics, you may store them casually in open storage, but I like keeping them in a cabinet of some sort—it's nice to have all your linens in one place. I try to use pure cotton and linen because they are easy to throw in the washer and dryer. I prefer a worn, wrinkly look to my linens, but if that bothers you, you'll have to iron them before folding them up and storing them in the cabinet. (And if you have very fine linens, they should be laid flat, preferably wrapped in acid-free paper, and rolled instead of folded, to prevent permanent creasing.)

WALL DECORATIONS

I wish we had more wall space in our apartment so we could display more art. Our space for wall decorations is especially limited because we like to leave one white wall completely blank so we can project movies onto it (a favorite activity in our family). The wall next to the kitchen, however, has become a sort of collage of art. It's an ongoing process; little by little, I've added a mixture of artworks and photographs in different frames. I find the frames, new and used, at flea markets and dollar stores. I like the fact that they don't all match—it makes for a more interesting and alive display.

I like to hang different objects on the wall—not just pictures or photographs. I've used decorative ceramic plates and a sweet little wreath made out of birch bark. I also favor hanging textiles on the wall. You can simply pin them up for an evening or so and then take them down when you want to change up the arrangement.

FLOWER ARRANGEMENTS

As a designer, I get a lot of inspiration from plant life and flowers, so it's only natural that I like to have floral arrangements in my house. Back in Scandinavia, most people live very close to nature—we are rarely ever more than ten minutes from a beautiful park or a river, forest, field, or lake. Here in Brooklyn, I miss that proximity to nature, so I incorporate it into my designs wherever possible.

Flowers bring beauty and tranquility into our home. I tend to like plants that are simple in their looks and structure. My good friend Robb once commented on my designs, saying "You draw a lot of blobs on sticks." I suppose that is true. I also tend to like my plants like that: blobs on sticks. The simpler the better.

Many of the floral arrangements I make are not really "arrangements" at all: I simply place a branch or a flower in a vase. Don't overcrowd the vase; less is more.

I like to use everyday vessels rather than traditional vases in my flower displays. Many wine bottles have nice shapes and colors that work well in a grouping, for example. Or, why not use a mixture of drinking glasses, served up on a tray, and display them in the living room?

Placing a single branch or a stalk in a vessel gives a nice, clean look.

I always keep a few pots of herbs on my windowsill. I plant the herbs in basic terra-cotta pots, which I dress up with fabric. To make the "dresses," I use a tube of fabric with an elastic band sewn into the top and bottom, so the fabric fits the pot snugly.

Placing a few flowers in a bowl of water is another lovely way to make a simple arrangement.

I also like to play around with scale. Why do flowers always have to be above the top of a vase— why not keep the tops inside?

dried flowers : hang upride
down in a dark place

a single, small
tree branch

plant moss &
spring flowers
in bowls and
dishes

BEDROOM

Our bedroom is very minimalist. We hardly have anything on the walls. Both Nick and I work with visuals all day long and are constantly surrounded by information and visual input, so I try to avoid all of that in our bedroom. The bedroom is a place for rest, a place where the mind and body can unwind.

It is of course hard for me to stop myself completely. When it comes to bedding I do tend to pick fun patterns and colors. And I mix, rather than match!

QUILTS

Back in Sweden, we have a rich heritage of quilting, but it wasn't until I moved to the United States that I really became interested in quilts. When I saw the "Gee's Bend" quilts (Gee's Bend is a quilting style that originated after the Civil War in a rural community in Alabama) I just had to have them. They're so freestyle and creative—I love the imperfect and improvised look!

I must admit I am a rather impatient seamstress, and I'm not sure I can quite call myself a quilter, but I like the result of mixing together different fabric swatches. I sewed this blanket for our bedroom in a few hours. It was very fast, took zero planning, and it was a lot of fun.

I simply cut out a bunch of swatches and piled them up in one stack. Then I sat down by the sewing machine and started sewing them together one by one in a random order until I had several long rows of fabric. I then sewed all those rows together and they made up the quilt. It has a rather random, crooked look, but I like that; it feels like a collage and is unique and personal.

STORAGE

In our bedroom, we have two dressers. One is a nice midcentury design that I scored at the Salvation Army in San Francisco for forty dollars (I couldn't believe my eyes when I saw that price tag!), and the other is a very simple white dresser with lots of drawers from IKEA. I figured if I chose a white dresser it would look smaller and blend in with our white walls.

I am helplessly into patterns, as you've probably realized by now. I thought that adding some fun patterns to my dresser drawers would spice things up, so I lined them with pretty paper. If you are ambitious, you can print some lovely designs on matte craft paper, or you can find wonderful wrapping paper in any well-stocked crafts store. All you have to do is cut the paper so it fits on the bottom of your drawer, and place some double-stick tape between the paper and the bottom of the drawer to keep it from sliding around.

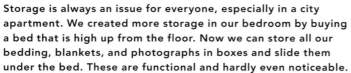

Storage is always an issue for everyone, especially in a city apartment. We created more storage in our bedroom by buying a bed that is high up from the floor. Now we can store all our bedding, blankets, and photographs in boxes and slide them under the bed. These are functional and hardly even noticeable.

I love these hooks that you can simply hang on the back of the door—that's such a dead space anyway, I figure I might as well take advantage of it. I use these hangers in almost every room in our apartment.

STENCILING

I like to have some really big, oversized pillows on the bed to lie back on when I am reading. For these, I had found some plain white twenty-four-inch pillowcases, and I created a simple stencil design for them.

This is a great project you can start and complete in one evening. It's easiest to print on cotton or linen. Keep the layout easy, and don't be afraid to play around with a two-color print.

While you have your stenciling tools and materials out, you might as well adorn a lampshade. The design shown here uses two colors, so it takes a little more time and patience to execute.

It's best to use an inexpensive lampshade made of linen or cotton. I recommend taping the stencil in place on the lampshade with some masking tape. That way it won't move around while you're stenciling.

First, stencil in the blue stalk and leaves. After that dries, stencil in the yellow flower. For the brown centers of the flowers, I used those furniture protection pads I recently discovered. They are sticky on one side, so you can simply plop them wherever you like. It couldn't be easier.

STENCIL

Step 1: Make the stencil

A: Draw your design onto the acetate or stencil paper with a permanent marker.

B: Using a craft knife and cutting mat or heavy cardboard, cut out your design, making sure to leave ample room around the motif to protect the fabric from accidental splashes. You will need to cut a separate stencil for each color used in the design.

1A

1B

Step 2: Print on the fabric

A: Pour a small amount of paint on to an old plate.

B: Place your stencil on top of your fabric. Secure the stencil to the material using masking tape so it will not move while you're printing. (This is why using self-adhesive plastic as a stencil is so handy; you don't need to secure the stencil with masking tape.)

C: Using a stencil brush or sponge, dab an even amount of ink through the stencil. Applying several thin layers of ink yields a better result than using too much ink at one time.

D: If you are printing more than one color, finish with the first before moving on to the next one. Let the ink dry before changing stencils. It is easiest if you have a separate brush or sponge for each color.

2 B

2 C

Supplies:
Acetate, or stencil paper
Permanent marker
Craft knife
Cutting mat or heavy cardboard
Paints and inks for fabric
Old plate
Fabric
Masking tape
Stencil brush or sponge

AUGUST'S ROOM

In a kid's room, you can really have fun with playful patterns and vibrant colors. In August's room, I let myself loose as far as mixing and matching goes. He doesn't seem to mind it (at least not yet).

I put up a wonderful textile piece
from Marimekko on the wall.
I simply hemmed it and pinned it up.

I made some floor cushions so August and I can comfortably sit and read together (and sometimes when we have several guests over, I bring these into the living room to use as extra seating). They are quite comfortable and make great accent pieces.

These fabric buckets are simple to make. They are sewn like a cylinder with a bottom, but you can play around with different shapes and sizes. I used lining and some fusing to add body and sturdiness to the sides. These are fun decorative accents that also serve the useful function of helping keep toys and doodads organized.

Contact paper is another household material I'm crazy about. It is so incredibly versatile. Here, I cut out some animal shapes to decorate the boring window shade we have in August's room. Contact paper is easy to remove, so if you get tired of it, simply peel it off and create a new design.

KITCHEN

When I was growing up in Sweden, we only went out for meals on special occasions. There are high taxes on restaurant meals there, so going out to eat has always been considered a luxury. Today this is starting to shift a bit, and more people are going out as international culinary influences make their way to Sweden and people become busier with work life and have less time to cook. But in general, Swedes are very hands-on and enjoy doing things themselves. Cooking is a central part of life, something we do every day.

Here in New York, people tend to be even busier, and time for cooking is limited. The options for takeout seem never ending! I admit it's a relief to order in on occasion, but cooking will always be a big part of my life.

I love to cook, and I spend as much time in our kitchen as possible. It may be tiny, but it is probably the most important part of our home. My cooking isn't overly complicated. I rely on simple methods and tricks I have learned over the years from my family and friends. My grandmother, Sylvia, was always cooking, and I spent a lot of time as a little girl helping her in the kitchen. My father used to be a fisherman, and he whips up amazing and delicious seafood recipes, which I've also learned to make myself. One of my favorite things to do is swap and share recipes with my girlfriends. I make sure there is always something new being thrown into the mix.

Travel has been another big influence on my cooking. Whenever I'm in a new place, I make a point to find the best local bakeries, restaurants, and markets. I always like to discover local specialty foods to bring home and try out in my own cooking (they earn bonus points if they come in unique packaging!). I like keeping my cabinets full of interesting and new ingredients from all over the world.

Recipes for some of my favorite dishes can be found on the recipe cards in the back of this book. (Since I have a weakness for baked goods, expect some cookie recipes as well—I couldn't resist!)

MAKING THE MOST OF SMALL SPACES

As I mentioned, we have a tiny kitchen; it's really just a few countertops and some cupboards. It faces out toward the living room area, which is actually nice because that way I can stir pots on the stove while conversing with my guests on the couch.

We use a rolling wooden cart to help separate the kitchen from the living room. It also serves as another much-needed countertop, and provides extra storage space for pots and pans.

When space is so limited, you have to work around things as best you can. I take advantage of every nook and cranny. Mugs, bowls, and appliances are stacked up and crammed together every which way, but somehow it works, at least for now. Besides, it gives our kitchen character!

When we moved into this apartment, the kitchen wall was covered with mirrors. It felt like something out of that 1980s TV series, *Dallas*. Needless to say, it was not really our style.

Since this apartment is a rental, we did not want to invest in retiling, so we solved the mirror problem with some contact paper instead. We chose a kitschy country motif that is vibrant and fun and livens up the kitchen area (much more than those mirrors did). It was challenging to apply the contact paper smoothly without any bubbles, but with some perseverance and patience we did it, and we're very happy with the results.

If you have a tiny kitchen like ours, don't be afraid to stack things on top of each other. I take advantage of every inch of storage space I can find. I keep glass bottles, thermoses, and baking tins on top of the kitchen cupboards, the refrigerator, and the microwave.

I found these really great spice tins that have magnetic backs, so they can be hung facing out on the side of the fridge. They are very handy and easy to grab. Keeping them there frees up more space in my drawers.

Isn't it funny how the fridge always seems to be the one place where people go totally crazy with photos, notes, and drawings? I love looking at my friends' fridge collages when I visit their homes. Decorating the refrigerator is a great way to personalize and liven up the kitchen, and it makes for a great conversation starter when you have guests over.

For storing dry goods, I use an array of attractive bins, jars, and boxes. They keep things organized, and they also look nice in the cupboard. I like to personalize them with my own hand-printed labels.

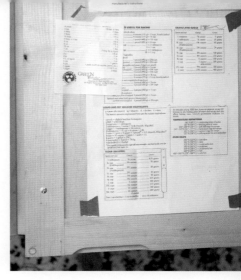

I use the inside of one of the kitchen cabinet doors to tape up favorite everyday recipes, notes, and measurement conversion tables.

In this cupboard, I keep my bowl collection. I have many different kinds of ceramic and porcelain bowls—some of my own pieces, some that I bought in Japan, and some beautiful ones my mother-in-law made.

PERSONAL TOUCH

I say you cannot have too many kitchen towels (though my
husband strongly disagrees with me on this point). I am a
textile designer, and I keep my linen closet full of all kinds
of linens: midcentury ones from Sweden, pretty ones from
Japan, and of course the ones I make myself. I like to stencil
simple designs onto store-bought striped or checked towels.
It's easy to do and is a great way to add a personal touch to
purchased items. They also make great hostess gifts (if you
are like me and aren't allowed to keep any for yourself).

I like to apply stencils to
swatches of industrial wool to
create durable potholders and
trivets. You can make any size
you need—a really big one for a
stockpot or a smaller one for a
little teapot.

Hand-stenciled dish towels

Next to the stove, I hang my trays in a "tray sling." These were quite popular in Sweden about forty years ago. You don't really see them much today, but I like them because they are fun, practical, and help keep things stored and organized. Plus, they are easy to make! Simply make two fabric bands (approximately 2 to 3 inches wide) and sew them into loops. Before you sew them up, thread both loops through a wooden ring. Once you have sewn the loops closed, hang the sling on the wall by the wooden ring. Make sure that the fabric bands are long enough when finished to hold your biggest tray.

Another great way to add your personal touch to your kitchen is to decorate your own glassware and plates. There are tons of fabulous paints and inks that are food and dishwasher safe (see Resources for some suggestions).

I tend to be spontaneous with my designs and simply draw doodles and motifs directly on the item I'm decorating. But some designs do look better if you give them some thought and plan them out on a piece of paper first.

These projects make excellent birthday and holiday gifts, and offer an easy way to update your cupboards with unique designs of your own.

COOKING

Cookbooks are another thing I cannot stop collecting. I buy them constantly, and I also have all my mother's and grandmother's cookbooks. Some of them are falling apart, but I will never get rid of them. They are far too precious.

I also keep a black notebook handy, and I jot down my favorite new recipes. Over the years, I've collected quite a few—things I've tried or recipes I've learned from other people. It is my own personal cookbook.

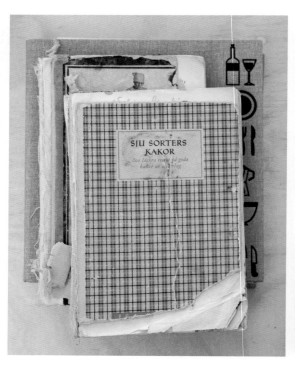

SUNDAY PANCAKE

One of my family's favorite recipes from the notebook is for pancakes. The recipe is from Åland, where I was born, and is simply called "Åland pancake." It is made from leftover porridge, baked in a deep casserole dish, and served with a prune compote or raspberry jam. It is a little taste of home. We often eat it for dessert, but it works for Sunday brunch as well.

PRUNE COMPOTE
Sviskon Kräm

This prune compote is delicious on the Sunday Pancakes, on
any other breakfast bread, or eaten in a bowl with milk.

APPLE JAM
Äpple Marmelad

I make apple jam every fall. It is a family tradition. The recipe comes from my friend's mother, Ingrid, who has been making this jam for years. I remember going to Maria's house when I was growing up and always hoping her mother would serve me some of this jam on a sandwich. She shared the recipe with me, and now it is one of my favorite things to make. It's great served with hot cereal or toast for breakfast, or with a soft cheese, like brie, as an appetizer. Every year I whip up a big batch and preserve it in glass jars; these make sweet and lovely holiday gifts.

SPRINGTIME MEAD
Mjöd

On the evening of April 30, many Swedes and other Nords celebrate the holiday of *Valborgmässoafton* (Walpurgis Night). They light a big bonfire and gather around and sing songs to celebrate the arrival of spring.

It is common in some parts of Scandinavia to serve mead and funnel cakes on this evening. I remember my grandmother making mead and storing it on her tiny balcony to keep cool. A fridge would have been too cold, but the cool air on the balcony was just the perfect temperature.

As a little girl, I used to gulp this stuff down—don't worry, there actually isn't much alcohol in it. It's more like a fizzy lemonade, with a little kick. Well, many years later, I decided to pick up this old tradition, which had sort of been forgotten in our family. I started making mead, and it was a huge hit. It is delicious, refreshing, and very easy to make. All you need are lemons, water, sugar, and some yeast.

ENTERTAINING

We really enjoy having people over to share some nibbles or a meal, sip some drinks, and share stories and laughter. On weekends especially, we like to entertain—it might be a sit-down dinner for four, a coffee or cocktail hour for twelve, delivery pizza with our best friends, or a party with forty people or more. Believe it or not, we have served a turkey dinner for ten people around our dinner table (it was tight, but it worked!). We keep extra folding chairs in the closet and pull them out for dinners or parties. It doesn't matter that we have a rather small apartment. When it's party time, we cram people in and everyone has a great time.

My Scandinavian heritage really comes out in the food I prepare for special occasions and holidays—pickled herring, sweet treats, and tons of casseroles. In this section, I'll share some of my favorite traditional meals with you to give you a taste of how we celebrate the holidays in our home. You'll also find some simple tips and handmade crafts projects to help you create a lovely table setting that will make a lasting impression on your guests.

FIKA

Fika is a social institution in Sweden. It means having coffee with colleagues, friends, or family—and boy, do we fika all the time! Swedes are actually among the heaviest consumers of coffee in the world.

A fika can be in the morning, midday, or afternoon. It's just a time to take a break from whatever you're doing, meet a friend, and share some coffee and cookies, buns, or biscuits. I keep this tradition alive here in Brooklyn and meet up with my good friend Annika every week for a fika.

I'm lucky to have a little balcony at the back of the apartment —and when I say little, I really mean little. It is about the size of a stamp, but it is just big enough for a table for two. We like to have coffee, breakfast, or early evening drinks out here, and we have a little mini barbeque that we fire up on warm summer nights. Living in New York, it's a treat to have an outdoor space with some plants and greenery, a few herbs, and a little bit of a view. We face out toward the backyards of our neighbors and see a lot of laundry hanging to dry—a classic Brooklyn view, I think, and one I love!

CINNAMON BUNS
Kanel Bullar

Like most Scandinavian kids, I grew up on cinnamon buns. As a little girl, I spent hours with my grandmother rolling out dough. Now, as a mother myself, I have to pony up and make these for August. It's his birthright, after all! Plus, they make the house smell wonderful and add a special touch to any fika.

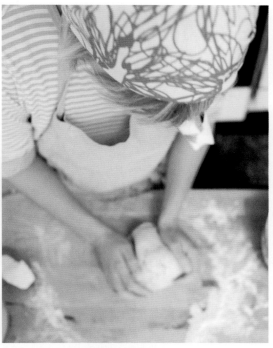

Cinnamon buns require a little bit of a time commitment, because there are many steps. It's best to make a big batch, so you can freeze leftover buns for later.

These chocolate slices are another classic Swedish cookie with rich, irresistible chocolate flavors.

Vaniljbågar cookies are another great fika treat. They're made with a lot of butter and melt in your mouth.

BIRTHDAYS

For my last birthday, I decided to make *smörgåstårta,* a popular Scandinavian dish usually served at festive occasions like birthdays and christenings.

It is literally a "sandwich cake," made up of several layers of white bread with creamy fillings between them, topped with various things like eggs, prawns, ham, paté, or caviar. It may sound strange at first, but it is very good served with a cold glass of beer or white wine, I promise.

For the party, I set the table with some of my favorite linens and these really interesting fabric napkins I found at Ikea. I had gotten this stack of gold-rimmed plates at a local flea market just days before, and they were perfect for the occasion!

This was a smaller birthday party, so I had time to give it a personal touch. First, I made some unique origami-style handmade invitations. Then I made place cards for each guest using rubber stamps and thick paper. I wanted to give the place settings a little kick, so I went for hot pink.

KALAS

annat:

serverter
bubbligt
vin
prosecco

räkor
gurka
majonäs
vatten
alkoholfri dricka?
fröken
vitpeppar-hl
citron
dill
lök
potta till August

gör en inbjudnings
lista

kaffe
småkakor
grädde
serpintinar

Using permanent marker pen and clear acetate paper; trace this flower shape

Cut out the flower = this is now your mold.

Use your mold to mark the

Fold the flower shape along the dotted lines

flower shape on the paper you want to use for your invitations.

HOLIDAYS

Every December we throw a holiday party for family and friends. We make some of my favorite holiday dishes from the Old Country, and set up a nice buffet table.

For this party, I like to keep the decorations simple and classic. You won't find many little elves or angels around our house, but you will see plenty of festive paper mobiles and candles to create a cozy atmosphere.

For the past few years I have used a nice branch with berries as a centerpiece, and I've decorated ginger cookies to use as tree trimmings. The traditional Christmas tree hasn't played a significant role in our home, but I'm sure now that we have August, we'll start that tradition very soon.

HOLIDAY DECORATIONS

As you know, I am very fond of industrial felt. It is such an easy material to work with, and it makes a lot of sense to use it around the holidays because it is so soft and fuzzy. It makes nice wintry decorative items.

Last year, I cut out some holiday flowers and placed them everywhere around the house. (Even Webster, the cat, got adorned! That lasted for all of two minutes.) I made a wintry pillow from off-white wool and glued the felt flowers to one side with textile glue. Felt flowers like these also can serve as adorable little coasters or adornments to placemats. Just cut them out of felt with sharp scissors and attach them with a dab of textile glue to a placemat or pillow cover.

I also like to hang simple paper mobiles as decorations. To make these, cut long, thin strips of paper in different colors (I generally use different shades of gray, cream, and white, but of course you can use any color you want). Bring together the ends of the paper strips to create a round loop, and secure them with some glue or an itsy-bitsy piece of tape. Keep adding more circles to create a ball by layering circles over each other. Once you have created a few of them, string them together using a needle and cotton thread.

HOLIDAY RECIPES

Gravlax
Gravad Lax

The most important food item on my Christmas table is probably gravlax. Scandinavians are surrounded by water and have access to all kinds of fresh fish, so it's no wonder we love our seafood. Gravlax is a festive and economical way to prepare a nice piece of salmon. I have tried many kinds of gravlax in many different countries and at several smorgasbords, and I have never tasted any better than the one my dad makes! He is simply a natural at this, and I try very hard to imitate him. The recipe for our gravlax is quite easy actually. Served with its special sauce, it is sure to be a hit on any holiday table. Give it a try!

I leave the thin slicing of the gravlax to my husband, Nick, who seems to enjoy the process immensely. We make a great team!

No Scandinavian Christmas dinner table is complete without pickled herring and potatoes! Eat the herring and potatoes together in one delicious bite or serve the herring on crisp bread.

Meatballs
Köttbullar

Swedish meatballs are another classic dish I love to serve. I couldn't do a holiday party without them! I serve them at room temperature with either mustard or lingonberry sauce. I can't tell you why Swedish meatballs have gotten such a stellar international reputation. Many cultures have meatballs; why are ours so famous? They are not very spicy (no garlic in sight!), but they are definitely delicious. My grandmother Sylvia made the best meatballs I have ever tasted. She simply had the touch!

Gingersnap Cookies
Pepparkakor

As I mentioned earlier, gingersnap cookies make fun decorations.
But they also are a delicious addition to your holiday meal. They are
almost a "must" in Swedish homes during the holidays.

You can pair them with blue cheese (a surprisingly good combo)
as an appetizer, or serve them together with a cup of hot glögg, a
traditional holiday drink.

Glögg

I start sipping hot glögg in the beginning of December to put me in the holiday mood. It is sweet and warm, and it smells so good. (The best part is, if you spike it, it gets even tastier!)

We like to serve a good Swedish snaps (or two) to get the insides warm and relaxed. We usually pair it with some beer and a song and serve it with food during the holiday meal.

Jansson's Temptation
Jansson's Frestelse

This dish is like a potato gratin, but with anchovies added. It is a thick, creamy, and delicious casserole, and it's always a hit at my parties. It can be served at room temperature, and it tastes great with a cold beer!

AT WORK

AT WORK

I am fortunate enough to have my own office that I can decorate however I like. Since I spend a lot of time in this space, I also spend a lot of time decorating and reorganizing it.

    I don't feel that my work is something separate from me; how I work and what I do is simply an extension of who I am. And since I love my work, it's only natural that I want to create a workspace I love as well.

    Because I spend so much time here, my office has become my second living space. I have a kitchen and a couch and coffee table there. It's a place where my ideas and thoughts take shape, so I make sure it is comfortable and filled with things that inspire me.

The studio is painted all white; my designs and sketches work as color accents. I buy functional furniture and create several workstations for different projects, and I make sure I have a lot of storage. Storage is key for keeping things organized and minimizing distraction.

INSPIRATION AND ORGANIZATION

I gather inspiration everywhere. I keep sketchbooks and collect drawings and magazines, and I have innumerable clippings and photographs. I use all these on a big wall in my studio to make a constantly changing collage of images and motifs that inspire me. I call it my inspiration wall.

I'm also in the habit of tearing out pages from magazines and keeping them in plastic sleeves in simple binders I get from the office supply store. These notebooks have become another resource for inspiration, and I refer back to them often for mood, color, or layout ideas.

I own tons of books as well, but I don't have a system for organizing them yet. I think putting them in order according to subject matter might be best, but I'm tempted to organize them simply by size.

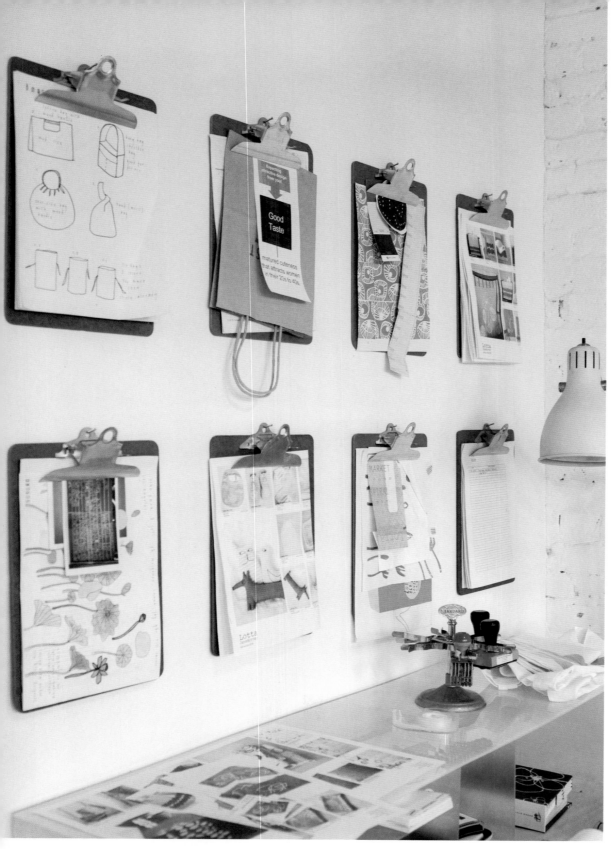

I've become fond of these old-fashioned clipboards, which I find
at yard sales and flea markets (you can also buy new ones in office
supply stores). I've hung a whole row of them above my desk,
and I clip price lists, shipping info, phone numbers, and magazine
cuttings to them. They're not only useful, they're also a clever
decorative idea.

I use all kinds of unusual containers to organize things in my office—ceramic planters, silver and wooden bowls, little trays, and so on. All these things look cute in an office and are great for holding tools, office supplies, business cards, or merchandise. Storage doesn't need to be boring—you can get creative and use all kinds of containers to hold things.

in construction

the first time I saw
my new   studio space

an old knitting
factory

painted all white   new

floors - a clean slate ...

measuring and

cleaning

planning

...but not for long

slowly getting settled

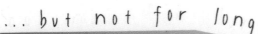

- moved in !

Painted the whole studio white- a clean canvas to work

OC	OC-57	white heron	OC-58	white ice	OC-59	vanilla milkshake	OC-60	icicle

with and to add to!

OC	OC-37	glacier white	OC-38	acadia white	OC-39	timid white	OC-40

stay calm

GET CREATIVE

I always keep my eyes open for pieces of furniture that would be easy to reupholster. I am not all that savvy in this area, so for me, they have to be very easy projects. But it's really fun to make customized office chairs or sofa cushions just using a good staple gun and sewing a few seams. For more involved upholstery projects, you can, of course, get professional help (I have done that many times myself!). It will set you back a few bucks, but it's worth it to have one-of-a-kind furniture pieces in your home or office.

In the studio, we've created a separate area for meetings and lunch breaks. We placed a shaggy rug under the sofa and coffee table to define the space and make it feel cozy.

I have a nice long wooden bench on which I store magazines. Underneath it I stash notebooks and folders. When necessary, I remove the magazines and use the bench as extra seating.

In the "shop" section of my studio, we've hung tote bags on a wall as a display. I took a very loose approach to the layout, and arranged the hooks randomly for a laid-back look. If you have a free wall at home, you can easily replicate this; just hang some hooks for all your bags. This would make sense in a hallway, or on a wall in (or close to) your closet. It's a creative way to organize, and a fun way to display all your pretty bags and purses.

In most offices, workspace can be limited. If you need an extra surface or desk, it's easy to put together sawhorses and a tabletop (simply cut from a sheet of plywood). These makeshift desks are very sturdy, and when you're done using them, you can simply fold them up and store them.

Here's an idea for a cheery mobile for the office: cut leftover paper scraps into almond-shaped pieces, then string them together with a sewing machine.

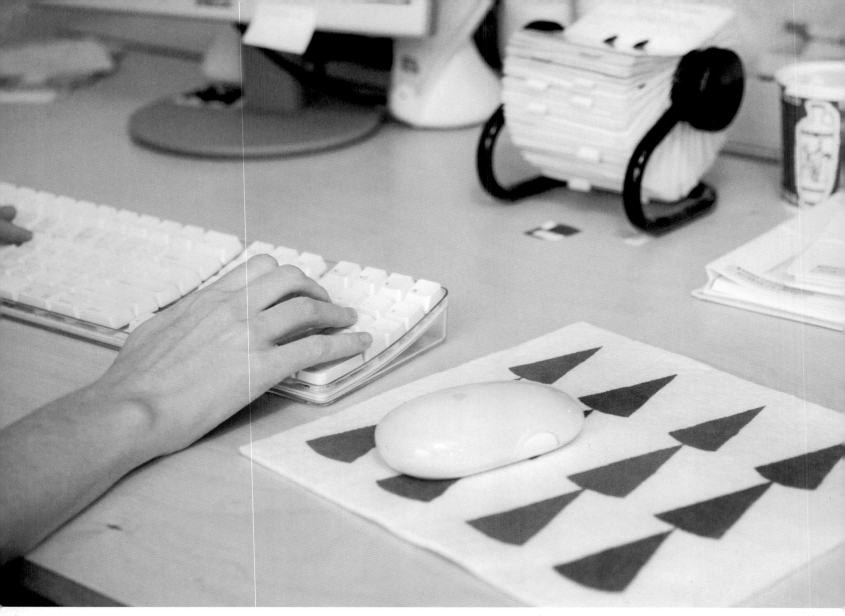

For my desk, I made a wool mouse pad decorated with some simple stencil prints. All you need to make a pad like this is a rectangular piece of wool, stencils, and fabric paint. It will liven up your desk and give it personal style.

In one of my windows, I hung some fun test-tube vases I created. To make these, simply sew some little cases out of fabric and fit them around test tubes. Then hang them with fishing line, and fill them with sprigs or flowers.

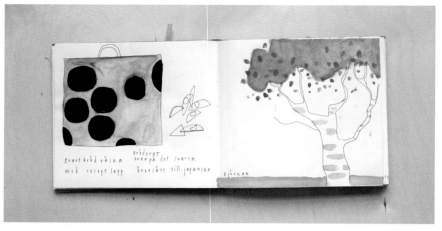
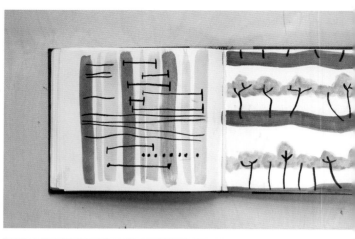

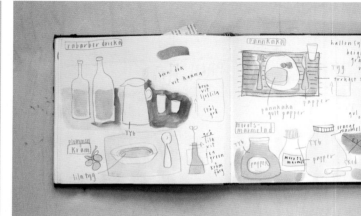
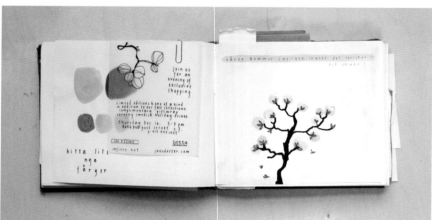
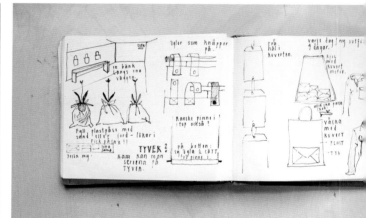
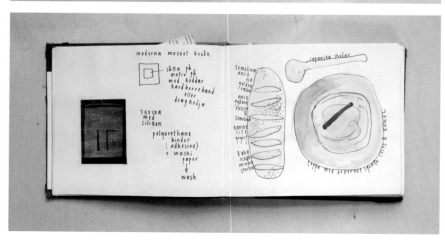
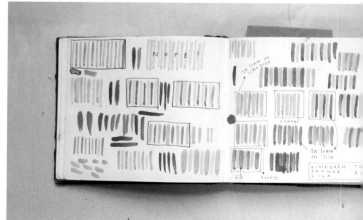

CONCLUSION

In this increasingly busy and chaotic world, our homes are the
one remaining place where we're allowed personal expression—
a place where we can just be ourselves and relax. I hope this visit
to my home and office has inspired you to start creating your
own comfortable and peaceful living and office spaces. As the
saying goes, "There's no place like home."

Thank you for the visit!

RESOURCES

If you want to learn more about what I do, please visit my Web site: **www.jansdotter.com**. Here you will find fabric kits, fabric swatches, stationery, labels, totes and bags, prints, items for your home, and more books. For printing and stenciling, I have a great printmaking kit and also a portfolio filled with stencils and original Lotta Jansdotter designs.

Following, you'll find lists of resources to help you track down beautiful home décor items and lots of contemporary Scandinavian designs.

GENERAL MERCHANDISE

Rakks carries lots of great shelving, including the shelves we have in our home.
www.rakks.com

The Sweden Shop is a great resource for Scandinavian accessories.
www.theswedenshop.com

Modern Seed carries sweet and modern decorating and lifestyle items for your child.
www.modernseed.com

Oeuf offers a wonderful line of goods for little ones.
www.oeufnyc.com

Scandinavian.Modern provides great vintage Scandinavian furniture and accents.
www.scandinavianmod.com

UNIQUE AND HANDMADE ITEMS

Here's a list of fabulous independent artists and designers who have created some of my favorite ceramic vessels, plates, and unique decorative items:
www.raedunn.com
www.dianafayt.com
www.sherryolsen.net

Bishop Lenno hand-paints the small, cute painted letter canvases that you can see on page 59 in this book.
www.bishop-art.com

LINENS

Some of my favorite linens—simple, useful, and high-quality—can be found at **www.foglinenwork.com**

Fabulous hand-crafted textile designs and fabric items are available from **www.judyrosstextiles.com**

CRAFTING SUPPLIES

You can find all sorts of craft supplies and paints at:
www.pearlpaint.com
www.joann.com

Virginia Johnson offers sunny, happy, and vibrant fabric designs (along with some fabulous clothes and totes).
www.virginiajohnson.com

Denyse Schmidt is an incredibly talented designer and quilter with a modern take on old techniques. Her Web site offers great fabric and scrap bags.
www.dsquilts.com

Amy Butler's designs are colorful and inspiring. Visit her Web site to find retailers that carry her fabric.
www.amybutlerdesigns.com

Paula Smail is inspired by Japanese gardens, trees, and her travels. Her fabric is perfect for smaller projects or quilts.
www.henryroad.com

Anna Maria Horner showcases sweet florals and pretty patterns.
www.annamariahorner.com

My mother used Marimekko for nearly all of her projects, so I grew up with this fabric all around me. I used Marimekko for many of the projects in the book. Find their beautiful fabrics online.
www.kiitosmarimekko.com

Modern, retro-inspired fabrics created by a husband-and-wife team out of Brooklyn.
www.twenty2.net

For your felt projects:
www.aetnafelt.com

FOOD

Luckily, now I do not have to schlep a bunch of coffee and herring from Sweden. I can simply shop all my traditional food cravings on these Web sites—and so can you:
www.northerner.com
www.swedensbest.com

At Ikea, you can find most of everything: great fabric by the yard, pillow blanks to print on, glass and ceramics to decorate, jars, storage bins, and a gazillion other cost-effective items for your home! This is also a very good place to find some of the Swedish food items that I mention in this book. Go online to find a store close to you.
www.ikea.com

INSPIRATION

My Favorite Magazines:
British *Elle Décor*
Inside Out
101 woonideeen
MILK

Lifestyle and Décor Blogs:
hopingforhappyaccidents.blogspot.com
www.grijs.blogspot.com
bloesem.blogs.com
swissmiss.typepad.com

Design and Lifestyle Books on my Bookshelf:
Arranging Things by Leonard Koren
Brooklyn Modern by Diana Lind
Clear Your Clutter with Feng Shui by Karen Kingston
Denyse Schmidt Quilts by Denyse Schmidt
Finnish Summer Houses by Jari and Sirrkkaliisa Jetsonen
Guide to Easier Living by Mary and Russel Wright
House Comforts: The Art and Science of Keeping House by Cheryl Mendelson
Quilts of Gee's Bend by Tinwood Books
San Francisco Kitchens (a Japanese book, published by edition Paumes)

Music that inspires me:
These are some of my favorite albums that I never get tired of listening to.

All You Can Eat, KD Lang
Bande a' Part, Nouvelle Vague
Beautifully Human: Words and Sounds, Vol.2, Jill Scott
Brazil Classics 1: Beleza Tropical, compiled by David Byrne
Breakfast at Tiffany's, Henry Mancini
Brown Sugar, D'Angelo
The Cello Suites Inspired by Bach, Yo-Yo Ma
Collectors Series, Peggy Lee
Ella and Louis, Ella Fitzgerald & Louis Armsrong
Finally Woken, Jem
Hello Love, The Be Good Tanyas
The K&D Sessions, Kruder Dorfmeister
Live At Blues Alley, Eva Cassidy
Llama, Pepe California
Musings of a Telescopic Tree, Nerissa Campbell
Penthouse, Luna
Sign 'O' the Times, Prince
Simple Things, Zero Seven

And some Swedish Favorites:
Gyllene Blad ur Monicas Dagbook, Monica Zetterlund
Made in Sweden, Blacknuss All Stars
Med Sjal Och Hjarta, Svante Thuresson
Memories of a Color, Stina Nordenstam
Pool of Happiness, Anders Widmark featuring Sara Isaksson
Quell Bordel, Christian Falk
Sentimental Journey, Nils Landgren
Sing and Dance, Sophie Zelman
Söndag I Sången, Bo Kaspers Orkster
Stamning, The Real Group/Eric Ericson

And, finally, a place that always inspires me:
The Swedish Church
5 E 48th St.
New York, NY 10017
(212) 832-8443

If you ever find yourself in Manhattan, I encourage you to visit the Swedish Church on 48th Street. This is a calm haven in the middle of the crazy, hectic NYC pulse. Step into the library and enjoy a cup of coffee with a homemade cinnamon bun. It will soothe the soul!

INDEX

ÅLAND PANCAKE

(ÅLANDSPANNKAKA)

This rich and filling oven-baked pancake from the Ålandic Islands is made from leftover rice pudding or wheat cereal. The prune compote is a tasty and healthful topping.

Makes 6 to 8 servings

Prune Compote

2½ cups/625 ml water
10 prunes, pitted
1 cinnamon stick
3 tablespoons sugar, or to taste
1 to 2 teaspoons cornstarch mixed with 1 tablespoon water

Pancake

2½ cups Rice Pudding (recipe follows) or cooked farina (Cream of Wheat)
1 cup/250 ml whole milk
⅓ cup/90 g sugar
½ tablespoon salt
2 teaspoons freshly ground cardamom
1 large egg, beaten

Preheat the oven to 350°F/180°C. Butter a shallow 6-cup/1.5-l baking dish.

For the compote: In a medium saucepan, combine the water and prunes. Let stand for 30 minutes. Add the cinnamon stick and bring to a boil over medium-high heat. Reduce the heat to medium-low and cook until the prunes are tender, about 10 minutes. Stir in the sugar.

Stir the cornstarch mixture into the prunes. Cook over low heat for 2 to 3 minutes, or until thickened slightly. Remove from the heat. Serve warm, or let cool and reheat over low heat.

For the pancake: In a medium bowl, combine the rice pudding and milk. Stir to blend. Stir in the sugar, salt, cardamom, and egg until blended. Pour into the prepared dish and bake until golden brown, about 45 minutes. Remove from the oven. Cut into wedges and serve warm, with the prune compote.

RICE PUDDING
(*RISGRYNSGRÖT*)

In a large, heavy saucepan, combine 2 cups/500 ml water, a pinch of salt, 1 tablespoon butter, and 1 cinnamon stick. Bring to a boil and stir in 1 cup/220 g short-grain rice. Reduce the heat to low, cover, and simmer for 10 minutes. Add 4⅓ cups/1.04 l milk, increase the heat to medium-high, and bring to a boil. Reduce the heat to low, cover, and cook for about 30 minutes, or until the rice is tender and the liquid is absorbed. Stir in 1 tablespoon sugar (or more to taste) and serve warm.

MEAD
(*MJÖD*)

CINNAMON BUNS
(*KANEL BULLAR*)

A great beverage to quench your thirst on a hot summer day.

Makes six 750-ml bottles

17 cups/4.25 l water
¾ cup/185 g packed dark brown sugar
¾ cup/185 g granulated sugar, plus 6 teaspoons
Zest and juice of 2 lemons
¼ teaspoon active dry yeast
18 raisins

In a large stockpot, bring the water to a boil. Stir in the brown sugar, the ¾ cup/185 g granulated sugar, the lemon zest, and lemon juice. Remove from the heat and let cool to warm, 105°F to 115°F/40°C to 46°C. Stir in the yeast until dissolved. Let stand, uncovered, at room temperature for at least 12 hours.

Put 1 teaspoon granulated sugar and 3 raisins into each of six wine bottles. Strain ladles of the mead through a funnel into the bottles. Cap tightly with corks or bottle stoppers. Place in a cool, dark place for 1 to 2 days, until the raisins have risen to the surface. Store in the refrigerator until ready to serve.

Making these is a time commitment, but nothing tastes or smells better than freshly baked cinnamon buns. They are perfect with coffee, hot chocolate, or lemonade.

Makes 24 buns

1½ envelopes (4 teaspoons) active dry yeast
1 cup warm (105°F to 115°F/40°C to 46°C) whole milk
¾ cup/185 g granulated sugar
1 large egg, beaten
½ cup/125 g unsalted butter, melted
1 teaspoon salt
1 tablespoon ground cardamom
4 cups/630 g all-purpose flour

Filling

½ cup/125 g unsalted butter, at room temperature
½ cup/125 g granulated sugar
2 tablespoons ground cinnamon

Glaze

1 egg beaten with 1 tablespoon water
Pearl sugar for sprinkling

In a large bowl, sprinkle the yeast over the warm milk. Add a pinch of the sugar. Stir to dissolve the yeast, and let stand until foamy, about 5 minutes.

Add the remaining sugar, the egg, melted butter, salt, and cardamom. Stir until smooth. Gradually stir in the flour, ½ cup/75 g at a time, to make a smooth dough. Transfer to a floured board and knead for about 10 minutes, or until smooth and elastic. Transfer the dough to a lightly oiled bowl, turn the dough to coat it with oil, and cover the bowl with a damp kitchen towel or plastic wrap. Let the dough rise in a warm place until doubled, about 1 hour.

On a floured board, divide the dough in half and form each half into a ball. One at a time, roll each ball out into a rectangle 12 in/30 cm long and ½ in/12 mm thick.

For the filling: Spread half of the butter evenly over one rectangle of the dough. In a small bowl, combine the sugar and cinnamon; stir to blend. Sprinkle half of this mixture evenly over the dough. Roll the dough up lengthwise and cut the roll into 12 slices. Place the slices, cut-side up, on a baking sheet lined with parchment paper or in muffin cups lined with paper liners. Repeat with the remaining rectangle of dough and filling, placing the slices on a second lined baking sheet or 12 lined muffin cups. Cover each pan with a dry towel and let rise in a warm place until doubled, about 1 hour.

For the glaze: Brush the buns with the egg wash and sprinkle with the pearl sugar.

Preheat the oven to 400°F/205°C. Bake the buns until golden brown, about 8 to 10 minutes. Remove from the oven and transfer to wire racks to cool slightly. Serve warm.

VANILLA HORNS
(*VANILJ BÅGAR*)

CHOCOLATE SLICES
(*CHOKLAD SNITT*)

These buttery cookies are simple to make, and they're perfect for both festive occasions and morning coffee. It's amazing that so few ingredients can yield such delicate and irresistible cookies.

Makes about 3 dozen cookies

2½ cups/390 g all-purpose flour
1 cup/250 g cold unsalted butter, at room temperature
1 tablespoon vanilla extract
Sugar for coating

In a medium bowl, combine the flour and butter. Using a pastry cutter or two dinner knives, cut the butter into the flour until the mixture resembles coarse meal. Stir in the vanilla.

On a floured board, knead the dough lightly until smooth. Form into a ball, transfer to a resealable plastic bag, and refrigerate for at least 1 hour or up to 2 days.

Preheat the oven to 350°F/180°C. Butter two baking sheets or line them with parchment paper.

Divide the dough into three pieces. One at a time, use your hands to roll a piece into a rope about ½ in/12 mm thick. Cut into 3-in/7.5-cm lengths. Transfer a length to a prepared pan and bend into a crescent that is slightly thicker in the middle. Repeat with the remaining dough.

Bake until set but not browned, about 12 minutes. Remove from the oven and dip each warm cookie into a shallow bowl of sugar to coat. Transfer to wire racks set on baking sheets and let cool completely. Store in an airtight container.

This is another classic Swedish cookie, with rich chocolate flavor and sugar sprinkles. It will quickly become a favorite! The pearl sugar is available in cookware shops and online.

Makes about 3 dozen cookies

¾ cup/185 g unsalted butter, at room temperature
1 cup/250 g granulated sugar
2 cups/315 g all-purpose flour
¼ cup/20 g unsweetened cocoa powder
1 teaspoon baking powder
2 large eggs, beaten
1½ teaspoons vanilla extract

Pearl sugar for sprinkling

Preheat the oven to 400°F/200°C. Butter two baking sheets or line them with parchment paper.

In a large bowl, cream the butter and granulated sugar until light and fluffy. In a medium bowl, combine the flour, cocoa powder, and baking powder. Stir with a whisk to blend. Stir the flour mixture into the butter mixture until blended. Stir in half of the eggs and vanilla until smooth.

On a lightly floured board, form the dough into a ball, then divide into six pieces. Form each piece into a log about 3 in/7.5 cm in diameter. Transfer three logs to each prepared pan, placing them at least 1 inch apart. Flatten each log slightly. Brush each log with the remaining egg and sprinkle with the pearl sugar.

Bake for about 15 minutes, or until set. Remove from the oven and transfer to a cutting board. Cut each log into 1-in-/2.5-cm-thick diagonal slices while still warm. Transfer the slices to wire racks to cool completely. Store in an airtight container.

SAVORY SANDWICH TORTE
(SMÖRGÅSTÅRTA)

GRAVLAX
(GRAVAD LAX)

This layered sandwich with its creamy fillings is not only incredibly tasty, it is also a feast for the eyes and serves many guests.

Makes 8 to 12 servings

Salmon Filling

10 oz/315 g smoked salmon, chopped
½ cup/125 ml mayonnaise
⅔ cup/160 ml whipped cream cheese, at room temperature
1 tablespoon minced fresh dill
1 tablespoon grated fresh horseradish or prepared horseradish sauce, or to taste
4 hard-cooked eggs, shelled and chopped
Salt and freshly ground pepper to taste

Shrimp Filling

1½ lb/750 g cooked shrimp, shelled
3 oz/90 g caviar
1 tablespoon minced fresh dill
⅔ cup/160 ml mayonnaise
3 tablespoons whipped cream cheese, at room temperature

12 slices firm white bread (such as pullman loaf or French country-style bread), crusts trimmed
About 1 cup/250 g whipped cream cheese, at room temperature

Optional Garnishes

Thin slices smoked or marinated salmon rolled into roses
Cooked shrimp
Tomato slices
Lemon slices
Dill sprigs
Lettuce leaves
Caviar

For the salmon filling: In a medium bowl, combine all the ingredients and stir to blend. Taste and adjust the seasoning.

For the shrimp filling: In a medium bowl, combine all the ingredients and stir to blend.

Place a large sheet of plastic wrap on a work surface. Lay 3 slices of bread in the center of the plastic wrap and spread half of the salmon filling over the bread. Top with 3 more slices of bread and spread with half of the shrimp filling. Repeat with another 3 slices of bread to use the remaining salmon and shrimp filling. Top with the remaining 3 slices of bread. Press the torte lightly to compress, then wrap it tightly in the plastic wrap and refrigerate overnight.

Remove the plastic wrap and place the torte on a large serving platter. Spread the cream cheese evenly over the top and sides of the torte. Garnish with your choice of garnishes. Cut into slices to serve.

A festive, delicate fish dish that is always a hit. Serve it on its own or with a crisp bread. Choose fillets of similar size and shape.

Makes 4 to 6 first-course servings, or 2 to 3 main-course servings

2 salmon fillets (1 lb/500 g total), pin bones removed
2 tablespoons kosher salt
2 tablespoons sugar
2 tablespoons pepper
20 dill sprigs
Dill Sauce for serving (recipe follows)
Lemon wedges for garnish

Place one fillet in a casserole dish, skin-side down, and the second on a cutting board, skin-side down.

In a small bowl, combine the salt, sugar, and pepper. Stir to blend. Sprinkle the salt mixture over the flesh side of both fillets and rub it in. Place all the dill sprigs on top of the fillet in the dish. Place the other fillet on top of the dill, flesh-side down.

Insert the dish in a plastic bag and tie it closed with a twist tie. Put the dish in the refrigerator and place a heavy item, such as a cast-iron skillet or a brick, on top of the fish to weigh it down. Refrigerate for 12 hours. Remove the dish from the refrigerator and reverse the fillets, so that the top fillet is now on the bottom. Repeat to refrigerate the

fillets for a total of at least 48 hours or up to 72 hours (3 days), reversing the fillets every 12 hours. The fish will release some liquid, which helps to cure the fillets.

Scrape away the excess dill and spices. Pat the fish dry with paper towels and place each fillet, skin-side down, on a cutting board. Cut each fillet into very thin diagonal slices, removing it from the skin. Overlap the slices on a platter or individual plates and serve with the dill sauce alongside, garnished with the lemon wedges.

DILL SAUCE
(*GRAVLÅX SAS*)

In a small bowl, combine 1 tablespoon sugar and 1 tablespoon white wine vinegar. Gradually whisk in ⅔ cup/160 ml canola oil until emulsified. Season with salt and freshly ground pepper. Stir in 3 tablespoons minced fresh dill. Store covered in the refrigerator.

SWEDISH MEATBALLS
(*KÖTTBULLAR*)

GINGERSNAPS
(*PEPPARKAKOR*)

Swedish meatballs: an all-time favorite. Not too spicy or overly seasoned, these are the perfect "comfort food."

Makes about 50 meatballs; serves 8 to 10 as hors d'oeuvres

12 oz/375 g ground chuck
4 oz/125 g ground pork
3 tablespoons shredded or finely chopped yellow onion
¼ cup/15 g fresh bread crumbs
½ cup/125 ml half-and-half
1 large egg, beaten
1 teaspoon freshly ground white pepper
1 teaspoon salt, or to taste
Dash of ground allspice
2 tablespoons unsalted butter

In a large bowl, combine the chuck, pork, onion, bread crumbs, half-and-half, egg, pepper, salt, and allspice. Using your hands, mix together until blended. With wet hands, roll heaping tablespoons of the mixture into 1-inch-diameter balls.

In a large, heavy skillet, melt the butter over medium-high heat. Working in batches, add the meatballs and cook, shaking the pan as necessary to turn them, until browned all over, 8 to 10 minutes. Reduce the heat to low and cook a few minutes longer, until cooked through. Using a slotted spoon, transfer to one large or several small plates. Serve hot.

These cookies are tasty, sweet, and a holiday must! A tin of them makes a delicious gift.

Makes about 10 dozen cookies

1¼ cups/280 g packed dark brown sugar
1½ cups/375 g unsalted butter, cut into pieces
⅔ cup/105 ml light corn syrup
1 large egg, beaten
3⅓ cups/525 g all-purpose flour
1½ teaspoons baking soda
2 teaspoons ground cloves
Dash of ground cinnamon

In a large bowl, combine the sugar and butter. In a small, heavy saucepan, heat the corn syrup to boiling over medium-high heat. Pour the syrup over the sugar mixture and stir until the butter is melted. Let cool to room temperature. Stir in the egg until smooth.

In a medium bowl, combine the flour, baking soda, and spices. Stir with a whisk to blend. Gradually stir the flour mixture into the egg mixture to make a stiff dough. Transfer to a floured board and knead until smooth. Divide the dough in half, form the halves into two disks, place in a self-sealing plastic bag, and refrigerate overnight.

Preheat the oven to 400°F/200°C. Butter two baking sheets or line them with parchment paper. On a floured board, roll one of the disks ⅛ in/3 mm thick and cut into different shapes with cookie cutters. Place the cookies about ½ in/12 mm apart on the prepared pans.

Bake until set and lightly browned on the bottom, about 8 minutes. Remove from the oven and let stand on the pans for a few minutes. Using a metal spatula, transfer to wire racks to cool completely. Repeat with the remaining dough. Store in an airtight container.

GLÖGG

JANSSON'S TEMPTATION
(*JANSSON'S FRESTELSE*)

This traditional Scandinavian drink adds a little spark to the holidays. It is rather rich and sweet, so a little goes a long way.

Makes 6½ cups/1.6 l; serves 10

One 750 ml bottle dry red wine, such as Pinot Noir or Zinfandel
One 750 ml bottle port
2 cups water
1½ cups/375 ml Cognac, brandy, rum, or vodka
Zest of 1 orange, cut into strips
10 cardamom pods
2 cinnamon sticks
10 cloves
5 slices fresh ginger
Sugar to taste
10 teaspoons raisins
10 teaspoons blanched almonds

Combine the wine, port, water, Cognac, orange zest, and spices in a large nonreactive saucepan. Bring to a boil, reduce the heat to low, and simmer for 5 minutes. Remove from the heat and let cool. Cover and refrigerate for at least 12 hours or up to 24 hours.

Strain the mixture, then reheat over low heat (do not boil). Stir in the sugar and divide among 10 mugs. Add 1 teaspoon raisins and 1 teaspoon almonds to each mug and serve hot.

Rich and filling, this savory dish of scalloped potatoes with anchovies is a great addition to your holiday repertoire.

Makes 4 side-dish servings

8 to 10 white boiling potatoes (1½ lb/750 g total)
3 tablespoons unsalted butter
2 large yellow onions, cut into thin slices
2 cans anchovy fillets (about 4½ oz/140 g each)
1½ cups/375 ml half-and-half
½ cup/125 ml whole milk
¼ cup/15 g fresh bread crumbs

Preheat the oven to 400°F/200°C. Butter a shallow 6- to 8-cup/1.5- to 2-l baking dish.

Peel the potatoes and cut them into thin slices, putting them in a bowl of cold water as you go.

In a large skillet, melt 2 tablespoons of the butter over medium heat. Add the onions and sauté until golden, 5 to 6 minutes. Drain the potatoes and dry them in one layer between clean kitchen towels. Spread half of the potatoes in the prepared dish. Layer half of the sautéed onions on top of the potatoes in the dish. Add the remaining potatoes and top evenly with the anchovies. Layer with the remaining onions.

In a medium bowl, combine the half-and-half and milk; stir to blend. Pour this mixture over the potatoes. Sprinkle the bread crumbs evenly over the potatoes. Dot with the remaining 1 tablespoon butter.

Bake for about 45 minutes, or until most of the liquid is absorbed, the top is golden brown, and the potatoes are tender when pierced with a knife. Remove from the oven and let cool slightly before serving warm or at room temperature.

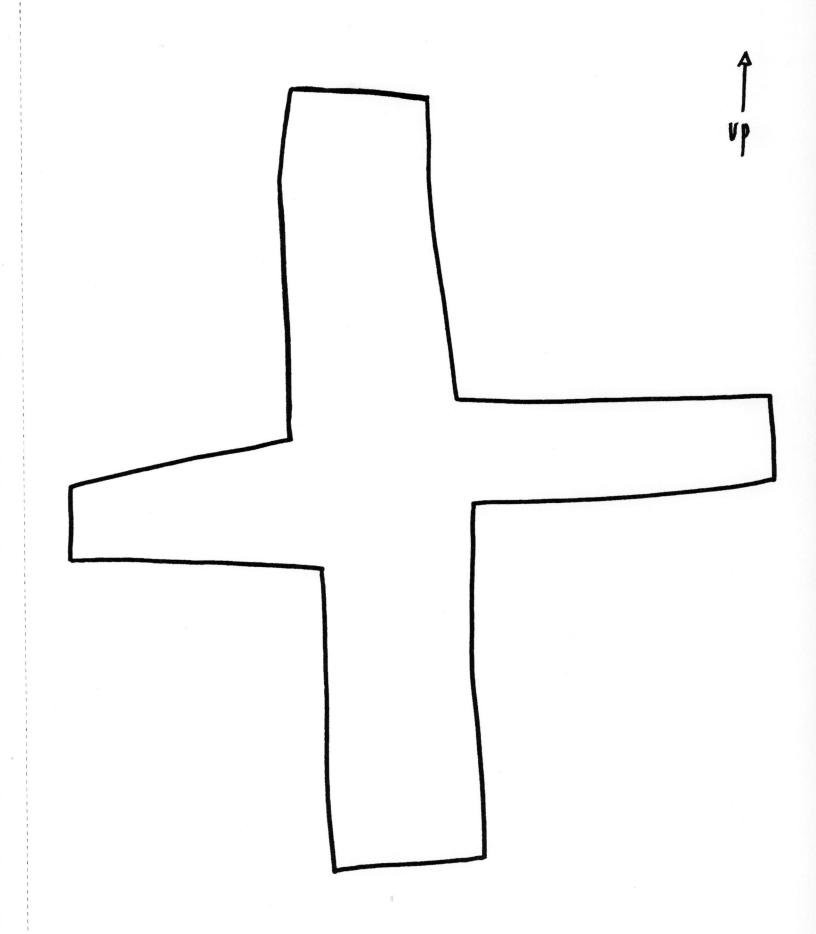

up

color 1

color 2

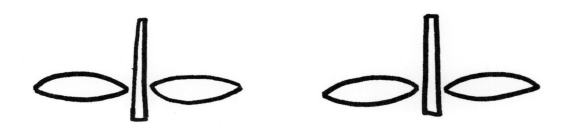

↑ up

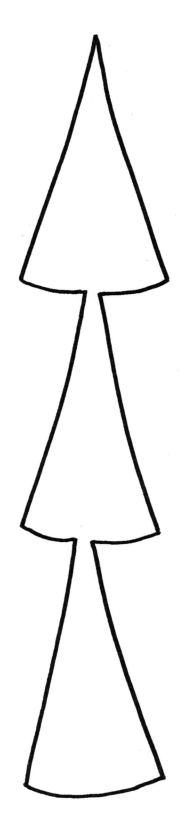
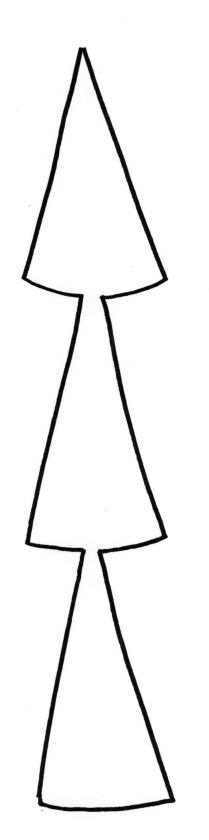